My dear readers,

Please forgive the flaws you may find in this little book. Because of the unusual times we live in at the moment and for the safety and health of all our neighbours and friends, I send this book out into the world naked and vulnerable. Without being able to receive a “Proof or Author’s Copy” I release this book, mistakes and all, to the gentle hands of you, dear reader. I ask for your understanding. I did my best for the moment and when I become aware of any mistakes, I will do my best to correct them as soon as possible. I ask for your kindness and understanding in this.

Thank you,

Kim West

What Your Heart Would Say to You

(if it could)

A small collection of heartfelt phrases
to let you know you are not alone

Book design by Walter Brunt

ISBN 978-1-9994668-8-6

This is dedicated to my dear husband.
I wish that I had met you earlier in life,
but I suppose if I had, I would never had needed
to hear the voice of my own heart.
Thank you for loving the me that I am.

A little about me?

"There is not much to tell about me, I often say. You see I am a very private person. I always show people that I am happy and well adjusted. It poses fewer questions from those around me. I don't want someone else to "fix" me. There is nothing "wrong" with me. I just seem to feel on a different scale than others. No one ever guesses that I have danced with the mistress of depression more often than I am willing to admit. That she lives in the corner of my mind ever hopeful that I will come back to her waiting arms. I love life I say to her. Life is full of beauty, of wonder, of multiple out comes, I say to her but she only shrugs and waits so I turn my back to her and go off to try and hear my heart. My heart knows me and holds my hand. My heart gives me strength to rise up to the day.

My story is my own so I will not share much of it with you, I am afraid, but I do know that we all have our own story and that is so much more important than my story alone. We are in this together. We are not alone. My heart acknowledges your heart and wishes you moments of peace and love. " - Kim West

Kim West has been a Joy Coach running her own life coaching company "The Positive Path - A Journey Towards Joy" for many years doing workshops, seminars and personal coaching for the purpose of bringing more positivity into our lives. In these times we can get bogged down with all that is negative in this world. Life becomes overwhelming and a struggle to see the positive in moments. There is more to life than just surviving the day to day routine we entrench ourselves in. We must try and remember all that is good, positive and even joyful so that we can live more fulfilling, balanced lives. Listening to our hearts is a good way to start.

A note about the pictures.

Most of my life, I have been trying desperately to hear the voice of my heart and I found that I was able to "hear" it best in places of beauty and solitude. There are many times though in our lives that we are not able to get up and go to a place where we can listen better and hear the messages that our hearts are trying to tell us, so I created an album of pictures I took in different places that reminded me of times when me and my heart were able to have a sit down. I tried to make this album feel like a dream state so that my inner eye and imagination would be engaged while using these pictures as a visual to help me meditate and clear my mind so I could "hear" better. These pictures were taken over decades with many different cameras. Some taken with actual film and developed, some with my professional camera and even some on my phone. These pictures were taken in White Horse, Haida Gwaii, Prince George, all over Vancouver Island, and all over the Okanagan. Everyone has a different place to go to listen to their heart but if you haven't found yours yet, you are more than welcome to use these as my gift to you. I am by no means a professional photographer, but I am an enthusiast, so each picture was taken with much intent from me... and my heart. Through these pictures I send good thoughts to you on your personal journey and wish only the very best for you.

Introduction

Now more than ever people are feeling alone, depressed and anxious. In these uncertain times there's so much pressure to be perfect, comparing ourselves to others.

We have all been there, but each of us goes through these moments of ups and downs differently. No one formula works for all. It's not a one size fits all solution. We all need someone who'll just hold our hand, listen and keep watch while we rest.

Our belief systems and faiths are all different, yet very much the same in the fundamentals of having someone who will look out for us. Having someone who is on our side carrying us through our hard times. Our hearts speak to us in those languages and through our hearts we can look beyond our trials, upsets and down times and see that there might be a way to survive. To get through this and get back to the path of our choosing.

This book gives a "voice" to our hearts. If our hearts could speak to us I am sure it would be lovely, and kind, and gentle with us. Letting us know that we are wonderful just the way we are and we are loved. During our dark times we sometimes feel that our hearts have betrayed us or abandoned us as it just sits there not saying anything, not helping us while we rage and rant and curse the sky for our upset state but I believe that it is just waiting until we are ready to hear its gentle whisper. When we are ready, then we will understand that our hearts were there holding our hand all along.

What Your Heart Would Say to You

(if it could)

I know it's hard to be strong right now,
but I know you can do it.

I know that you think that there is no good reason
for this to be happening to you, but I am here with you
and we will go through this together.

I am here for you.

I believe in you.

I know that it will take time for you to go through this.
I am here for you for as long as you need me.

I have no words that can make this go away, but just know that I am quietly by your side, always.

Just know that it is ok to feel this way.
I love you just the same.

Right now, I am giving you the best healing hug I can.

It's ok not to feel amazing right now.
I am right here no matter how you feel.

I will always be here no matter what.

Remember to take one step forward at a time.
You cannot go any faster than that.
I will hold your hand and we will take each step together.

I know that you are doing your best.
I am proud of you no matter what.

I know how brave you are and I am glad
to be on this journey with you.

Remember to think of one good thing a day.
I am by your side to help you celebrate the little things.

You are doing great. Keep going.
I am right beside you.

Focus on what and where you are right now.
I will help as much as I can.

Be kind to yourself. I think you are amazing.

Kim West 35

I am here for you, always.

I know that you are scared. I am right beside you and we will go through this together.

Tell me what you need and we can work toward making that happen for you.

It is ok to feel this way. You are you
and only you know how you feel.
I am here, if you need me.

I hear you and acknowledge what you have to say.

Take a deep breath and I will too.

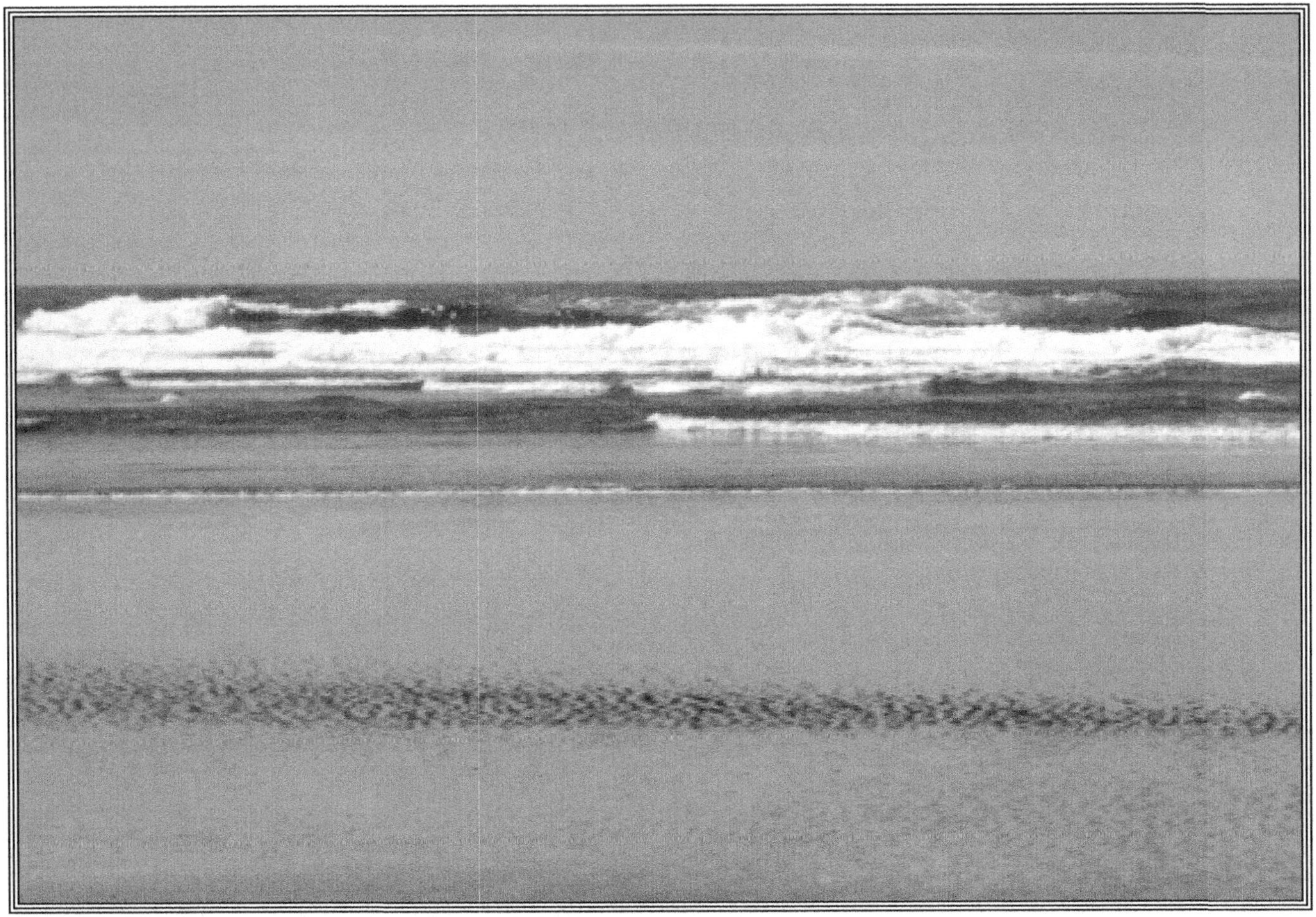

I am here to help you move forward.

I am listening. I hear you.

I am sorry that you are going through this.
I am here for you.

I care about you and always wish you well.

I know that you are hurting.
It's ok to feel this way.
Tell me all about it and I will listen.

We will go through this together.

I think that you are the most amazing person.

I will always walk by your side.

I am here to listen any time you like.

Tell me how you feel. I am here to listen.

It's ok to cry or feel upset.
I am here with you.

I am here to encourage you and to help
you on your own personal journey.

It's ok to feel small. I am as small as you
and we will do this thing together.

I don't know all the answers, but I will help you find the answers you need.

Be calm. We will stand in the moment of calm together.

Trust in yourself. I trust you.

It's ok if things are not perfect.
I am not perfect either.

I love you. No matter what.

Give me your worries and I will hold them
for a while for you.

You might not be ready right now,
but when you are, I am ready too.

Remember to look around you. I will help you to see where you are going.

I cannot fix everything,
but I will try and help where I can.

It's ok, you walked away from your path for a while.
I will always wait for you.

You are not alone. I am always here.

Remember that this is but a moment in time.
I am with you now and for all the moments to come.

You can do this. I know you can. I believe in you.

I appreciate you. I am happy to be by your side.

You are so courageous
to be taking the steps to move forward.
I am proud to see how far you have come.

Thank you for being you.
I am always amazed at who you are.

It is ok to take a little rest.
I am here and will keep watch for you.

It is ok to take a break
from learning something new each day.
When you are ready,
we will go back to learning together.

This might not be your ideal path,
but at least we will walk this path together.

Be patient with yourself.
I love you just the way you are.

It is ok to let go. Not everything has to be perfect.
I won't judge.

Let your mind have a rest from stress.
Tell me of a time when you were calm
and we will celebrate that together.

Listen to the quiet between the noise.
I will be still with you.

It's ok not to be the same person you were yesterday.
I like each version of you.

It is ok to think this sucks.
I hear you.

It's ok to stop and stand still for a moment.
I will stand with you.

Tell me how I can help and I will see what I can do.

I am sorry that you are feeling this way,
but remember it is ok to feel what you feel.

I know how hard this must be for you.
I am here to help, if you want.

I am here to support you.

I am here for you.
Let's take that step forward together.

You have a beautiful smile
that comes from your deepest place.
I love that smile
and will do anything to feel its warmth.

There are many beautiful things in this world.
Tell me about some and I will listen.

I understand how empty you feel.
I will do my best to help you feel fulfilled.

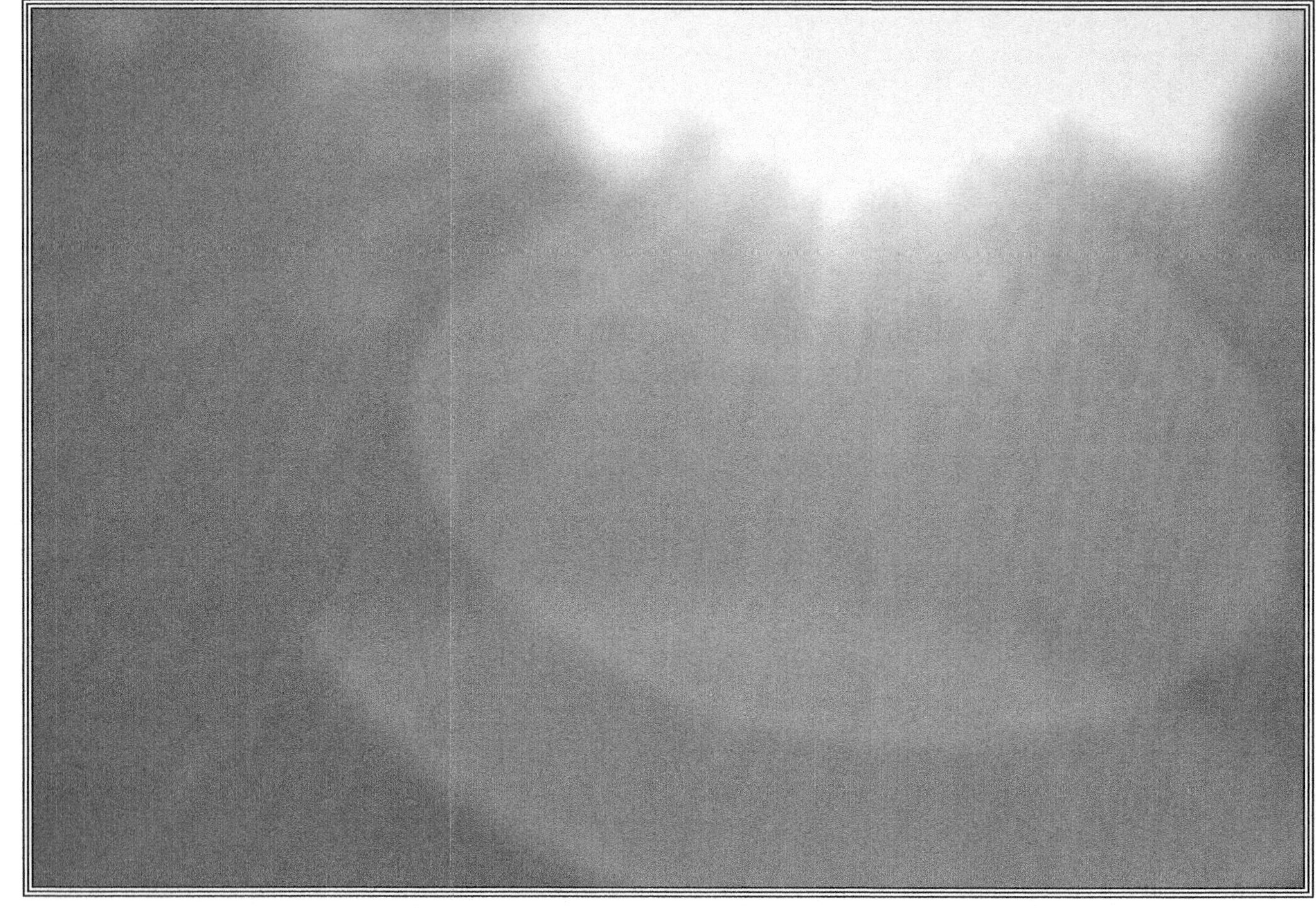

I am sorry that you are hurting.
I am here to help, if you want.

Tell me all of your worries and concerns
and I will listen to everything you have to say.

I will hold your hand and we will get through this.

I wish I can make this better for you.

I am always here to hear you.

You are doing the very best you can right now.
I am proud of you.

I wish you didn't have to go through this.

I understand that you are upset.
I am here to support you any way I can.

I will be with you until you feel better
then I will celebrate with you for feeling better.

I will do my best to hold the umbrella
while we weather this storm together.

I am here holding the light
so you don't have to walk in the dark alone.

I don't know what the answer is,
but I am here and we will find the answer together.

Take a moment and sit with me.
Everything will still be waiting for us
after we take a moment for ourselves.

I have known you since before time
and I know that you can do this.

If I could I would shield you from all that hurts you.

I know that you feel lost and unsure.
I am with you
and will do my best to guide you through this.

I always want the best for you
and I hope you know that I will always
be here for you.

Made in the USA
Monee, IL
19 November 2021